INSPIRING ARTISTS

FRANCISCO GOYA

Published in 2016 by The Rosen Publishing Group, Inc.
29 East 21st Street, New York, NY 10010

First Edition

Library of Congress Cataloging-in-Publication Data

Rockett, Paul.
Francisco Goya / Paul Rockett. -- First Edition.
pages cm. -- (Inspiring artists)
Includes index.
ISBN 978-1-5081-7058-7 (library bound)
1. Goya, Francisco, 1746-1828--Juvenile literature. 2. Artists--Spain--Biography--Juvenile literature. I. Title.
N7113.G68R58 2016
759.6--dc23
2015034932

Manufactured in the United States of America

INSPIRING ARTISTS
FRANCISCO GOYA

Paul Rockett

ROSEN
PUBLISHING®

New York

Picture acknowledgements: Front cover, 3, 11b; The Parasol, 1777. Museo del Prado, Madrid. Iberfoto/Superstock. Oil on linen, 104 x 152 cm. 4; The Third of May 1808, The Execution of the Defenders of Madrid, 1814. Museo del Prado, Madrid. Oil on canvas, 268 x 347 cm. 6t; Self Portrait at 69 years, 1815. Real Academia de Bellas Artes San Fernando, Madrid. Oil on canvas, 46 x 54 cm. 6b; Portrait of Ferdinand VII of Spain in Court Dress, 1814. Museo del Prado, Madrid. Fine Art Images/Superstock. Oil on canvas, 208 x 142.5 cm. 7t; Los Caprichos, No. 49, Duendecitos (Hobgoblins), 1799. Museo del Prado, Madrid. Etching & aquatint, 21.2 x 15.2 cm. 7b; Salvador Dali, Callagones de Cabra, No. 49 from Los Caprichos de Goya, 1977. © Salvador Dali, Fundació Gala-Salvador Dalí, DACS, 2015. Private Collection, published by Berggruen, Paris. Etching & stencil,18.4 x 12.7 cm. 8; The Victorious Hannibal Seeing Italy from the Alps for the First Time, 1771. Fundación Segas-Fagalde in Asturias. Oil on canvas, 87 x 131.5 cm. 9t; The Adoration of the Name of God, c.1772. Basílica de Nuestra Señora del Pilar de Zaragoza. Album Oronzo/AKG Images. Ceiling fresco. 9b; Giovanni Battista Tiepolo, The Apotheosis of the Spanish Monarchy, 1766. Palacio Real de Madrid. Paul Maeyaert/Bridgeman Art Library. Ceiling fresco. 10; The Blind Guitarist, c.1778. Museo del Prado, Madrid. Oil on canvas, 260 x 311 cm. 11tl; Blind Man's Bluff, c.1789. Museo del Prado, Madrid. Oil on linen, 269 x 350cm. 11tr; Tapestry by Livinio Stuyck y Vandergoten Real Fábrica de Tapices, Madrid, c.1800, after cartoon by Goya c.1789. Palacio de San Ildefonso, near Segovia. AKG Images. Wool and silk, 283 x 350 cm. 12bl; Christ on the Cross, 1780. Museo del Prado, Madrid. Oil on canvas, 255 x 154 cm. 12br; Anton Raphael Mengs, Christ on the Cross, 1761. Palacio Real de Aranjuez, Madrid. Album/Oronoz/AKG Images. Oil on wood, 198 x 115 cm. 13t; Diego Velázquez, Portrait of Sebastián de Morra, c.1645. Museo del Prado, Madrid. Oil on canvas, 106.5 x 82.5cm. 13bl; Diego Velázquez, Christ Crucified, 1632. Museo del Prado, Madrid. Iberfoto/Superstock. Oil on canvas, 249 x 170 cm. 13br; Sebastián de Morra, c.1778. Private collection. Etching, 20.8 x 14.9 cm. 14bl; Rembrandt van Rijn, Self-Portrait, Frowning, c.1630. Rijksmuseum, Amsterdam. Etching, 7 x 5.9 cm. 14br; Self-Portrait, c.1798-1800. Metropolitan Museum of Art, New York. Indian ink & wash on paper,15.2 x 9.1 cm. 15tl; Self-Portrait with Easel, c.1790. Real Academia de Bellas Artes San Fernando, Madrid. Peter Barrit/Superstock. Oil on canvas, 42 x 28cm. 15tr; Rembrandt van Rijn, The Artist in his Studio, 1628. Museum of Fine Arts, Boston. Oil on wood, 24.8 x 31.7 cm. 15br; Count Floridablanca, 1783. Banco de España Collection, Madrid. Iberfoto/Superstock. Oil on canvas, 260 x 166cm.16l; Don Manuel Osorio de Zuniga, c.1787. Metropolitan Museum of Art, New York. Oil on canvas, 127 x 101.6 cm. 16r; Charles III in Hunting Costume, c.1786-88. Museo del Prado, Madrid. Iberfoto/Superstock. Oil on canvas, 207 x 126 cm. 17l; Gaspar Melchor de Jovellanos, 1798. Museo del Prado, Madrid. Oil on canvas, 205 x 123 cm. 17r; Alice Neel, Frank O'Hara No. 2, 1960. © The Estate of Alice Neel. Private Collection. Oil on canvas, 96.5 x 61cm. 18bl; The Yard of the Mad House, c.1793-4. Meadows Museum, Dallas. Oil on tin-plated iron. 43.8 x 32.7 cm. 18br; The Shipwreck, c.1793. Private Collection, Madrid. Album, Oronoz/AKG Images. Oil on canvas, 50 x 32 cm. 19; Théodore Géricault, The Raft of the Medusa, 1818-19. The Louvre, Paris. Oil on canvas, 491 x 716 cm. 20bl; The Duchess of Alba, 1797. Hispanic Society of America, New York. Oil on canvas, 210 x149 cm. 21t; La Maja Vestida, c.1800. Museo del Prado, Madrid. Oil on canvas, 95 x 190 cm. 21b; John Singer Sargent, Madame X, 1883-4. Metropolitan Museum of Art, New York. Oil on canvas, 24.32 x 14.38 cm. 22bl; Henry Fuseli, The Nightmare, 1781. Detroit Institute of Arts. Oil on canvas, 101.6 x127 cm. 22tr; The Spell, 1797-8. Museo Lázaro Galdiano, Madrid. Bridgeman Art Library. Oil on canvas, 43.5 x 30.5 cm. 23; Witches' Flight, 1797-8. Museo del Prado, Madrid. Oil on canvas, 43.5 x 30.5 cm. 24bl; Los Caprichos, No. 39, And So Was His Grandfather,1797-99. Museo del Prado, Madrid. Etching & aquatint, 21.4 x 15 cm. 24br; Los Caprichos, No. 61, They Have Flown, 1797-99. Museo del Prado, Madrid. Etching & aquatint, 21.4 x 15 cm. 25t; Los Caprichos, No. 43, The Sleep of Reason Produces Monsters, 1799. Museo del Prado, Madrid. Etching & aquatint, 21.2 x 15.2 cm. 25b; Odilon Redon, The Dream of Caliban, (A Psychedelic Dream) 1895-1900. Musée D'Orsay, Paris. Erich Lessing/AKG Images. Oil on wood, 48.3 x 38.5 cm. 26; The Family of Charles IV, 1800. Museo del Prado, Madrid. Oil on canvas, 280 x 336 cm. 27; Diego Velázquez, Las Meninas, (La Familia de Felipe IV) 1656. Museo del Prado, Madrid. Oil on canvas, 318 x 276 cm. 28; The Colossus, 1812. Museo del Prado, Madrid. Oil on canvas,116 x 105 cm. 29; Robert Motherwell, Elegy to the Spanish Republic, No. 131, 1974. © Dedalus Foundation, Inc./VAGA, NY/DACS, London 2015. Detroit Institute of Art/Bridgeman Art Library. Oil on canvas, 243 x 304.8 cm. 30t; The Disasters of War, No. 44, I Saw It, 1810-20. Museo del Prado, Madrid. Etching & aquatint,16 x 23.5cm.30b; The Disasters of War, No 64,Cartloads to the Cemetery, 1810-20. Metropolitan Museum of Art, New York. Etching & aquatint,15.5 x 20.5 cm. 31; Pablo Picasso, Guernica, 1937. © Succession Picasso/DACS, London 2015. Museo Nacional Centro de Arte Reine Sophia, Madrid. Superstock. Oil on canvas, 349 x 776 cm. 32; Allegory of the City of Madrid, 1810. Museo Municipal Madrid. Bridgeman Art Library. Oil on canvas, 260 x 195 cm. 33t; The Second of May, 1808 (The Charge of the Mamelukes) 1814. Museo del Prado, Madrid. Oil on canvas, 266 x 345 cm. 33b; Eugene Delacroix, The Battle of Taillebourg 1242, 1837. Palace of Versailles. Peter Willi/Superstock. Oil on canvas, 489 x 554 cm. 34; The Third of May 1808, (The Execution of the Defenders of Madrid) 1814. Museo del Prado, Madrid.oil on canvas, 266 x 345.1cm. 35; Edouard Manet, The Execution of Maximilian, 1867. Kunsthalle Manneheim. oil on canvas, 252 x 305 cm. 36bl; The Burial of the Sardine, 1816. Real Academia de Bellas Artes San Fernando, Madrid.oil on wood, 82.5 x 62 cm. 36br; Los Disparates, No. 5, Disparate Volante, 1815-23. National Gallery of Art,Washington DC.etching & aquatint, 24.4 x 35.3 cm. 37t; Los Disparates, No. 4, Bobalicón, 1815-23. Museo del Prado, Madrid. etching & aquatint, 24.3 x 35.2 cm. 37b; Paula Rego, The Was A Man of Double Deed (Nursery Rhyme series), 1989. © Paula Rego, Courtesy Marlborough Fine Art. Leeds Museums and Art Galleries/Bridgeman Art Library.etching & aquatint, 32.5 x 21.6 cm. 38l; Self-Portrait with Dr Arrieta, 1820. Minneapolis Institute of Arts.oil on canvas, 42.13 x 30.12 cm. 38r; The Dog, 1820. Museo del Prado, Madrid.oil on canvas,131 x 79 cm.39t; A Pilgrimage to St Isidro, 1820-23.Museo del Prado, Madrid.oil on canvas, 140 x 438 cm. 39b;Edvard Munch, The Scream, 1893. The National Gallery, Oslo.oil, tempera, pastel and crayon on cardboard, 91 x 73.5 cm. 40t; I'm Still Learning, 1824-8. Museo del Prado, Madrid.Lithograph on paper,19.2 x 14.5 cm.40b; Bullfight in a Divided Ring, 1825. National Gallery of Art, Washington DC. Lithograph on paper, 29.5 x 41.3 cm. 41t;The Milkmaid of Bordeaux, 1825-7. Museo del Prado, Madrid. oil on canvas, 74 x 68 cm.41b; Camille Pissarro, The Shepherdess, 1881. Musée D'Orsay, Paris. Bridgeman Art Library/Superstock.oil on canvas, 81 x 65 cm. 42bl; The Little Giants, 1791. Museo del Prado, Madrid. Bridgeman Art Library.oil on canvas,137 x 104 cm. 42br; Two Old Men,1819-1823. Museo del Prado, Madrid.oil on canvas,146 x 66cm. 43; Ahmed Alsoudani, Untitled, 2010. © The Artist. Private Collection. Bridgeman Art Images.oil, charcoal and graphite on canvas,101.6 x 106.7 cm.

CONTENTS

First of the Moderns

Francisco Goya is celebrated as one of the greatest artists that ever lived. He is often referred to as the "last of the Old Masters and first of the Moderns," as he pushed the boundaries of traditional art into new areas. He developed a bold use of paint and recorded daring ideas and subjects, inspiring modern art movements.

A bursting talent

Goya was born in 1746 in Fuendetodos, a poor village in the Aragon region of Spain. His father worked as a gilder, and his mother was from an aristocratic family that had fallen on hard times. Goya's drive for success led him from these humble beginnings to life in the Royal Court, during which time he produced an enormous amount of work in many different art forms. His work includes tapestry designs, portraits, history paintings, church frescos and cabinet paintings, as well as etchings and lithographs.

Self-portrait at 69 Years, 1815

The Age of Enlightenment

As a professional artist, Goya painted all of the powerful people in Spain, even though he didn't always agree with the way they ran the country. Goya lived during the Age of Enlightenment (c.1650–1780), a time when traditional forms of power, such as the Church and the monarchy, were being challenged across Europe. But Spain was slow to modernize. Goya worked under three different Spanish kings; Charles III (reigned 1759–88), Charles IV (reigned 1788–1808) and Ferdinand VII (reigned 1808 and 1814–1833). Ferdinand VII in particular attempted to undo some of the Enlightenment's progress, including reversing checks that had been imposed on the king's power.

Portrait of Ferdinand VII of Spain in Court Dress, 1814

Religion

In the 15th century, the Spanish monarchy set up a special court called the Inquisition, which sought to protect Catholicism in the kingdom. It was also designed to punish anyone who might pose a threat to the monarchy. The Inquisition's presence in Spanish life greatly affected Goya. Privately he produced artworks that criticized them and other aspects of society, such as in the *Los Caprichos* series of prints (see p.24–25). In print *No. 49: Little Hobgoblins* (right) Goya shows the clergy as monsters. The central figure's sharp, jagged teeth and enormous claw-like hand refer to the powerful grip the Church had on the country.

No. 49: Little Hobgoblins, 1799

Major Modern influence

While Goya explored ideas of naturalism in his professional painting, his private work explored images of fantasy and self-expression. Both outlets allowed Goya to create masterpieces that are considered to be ahead of their time. His expressive use of materials and radical subject matter went on to influence many important artists and he blazed a trail for art movements such as Romanticism, Impressionism, Expressionism and Surrealism. Salvador Dalí (1904–1989) was just one famous Surrealist artist who was influenced by Goya's use of fantastical imagery. In 1973, 174 years after they were first made, Dalí drew over a set of Goya's *Los Caprichos* prints, making them appear even more fantastical in their depictions of life.

No. 49: Little Hobgoblins, Salvador Dalí, 1973.

Getting known

When Goya was still a child, his family moved to the nearby town of Saragossa. He began studying art at a local drawing school. Goya was an ambitious student, but it took a long time before he started to find success as a professional artist.

Apprenticeship

At the age of 14 Goya became an apprentice to the painter José Luzán (1710–1785). Luzán was a painter of religious art and Goya learned to paint and draw by copying his work in return for preparing Luzán's paints and canvases. After four years, Goya moved to Madrid, where he studied under Francisco Bayeu (1734–1795), a popular painter who worked at the Royal Court.

The Victorious Hannibal Seeing Italy from the Alps for the First Time, 1771

A trip to Italy

Goya wanted to continue his studies and applied twice for a scholarship at Spain's top art institute. Goya's applications were unsuccessful, and so sometime around 1770 he gathered his own funds together and left for Italy. Italy had long been the center of the art world and aspiring artists, like Goya, traveled here to study its rich history of painting as well as its practicing artists.

Competition

While in Rome, Goya entered a prestigious painting competition. He put forward *The Victorious Hannibal Seeing Italy from the Alps for the First Time* (below), a painting of the military commander Hannibal crossing the Alps into Italy. The painting was awarded an honorable mention. It showed the influence of Italian Rococo art, particularly of artist Giovanni Battista Tiepolo (1696–1770).

Rococo Tiepolo

Tiepolo was born in Venice in Italy, but spent the last few years of his life painting large frescos and altarpieces in Madrid, where he may have met Goya. Tiepolo was celebrated for

The Adoration of the Name of God, c.1772

his images of ancient myths and history. His paintings were typical of the Rococo style of art, which was rich with elaborate decoration and bursts of bright, light colors.

Back to Spain

Goya returned to Saragossa in 1771 and received his first major commission for a fresco in a local chapel. The fresco, *The Adoration of the Name of God* (above), shows groups of angels all facing toward a triangle with "God the Father" written inside in Hebrew. The work was a great success and helped to establish Goya's reputation as a professional artist.

Art

What similar features can you see in the painting by Tiepolo (left) and Goya's fresco (above)?

The Apotheosis of the Spanish Monarchy, Giovanni Battista Tiepolo, 1766

Tapestry designer

In 1773, Goya married Francesco Bayeu's sister, Josefa. Two years later they moved to Madrid, where his brother-in-law had found him work as a tapestry designer for the Royal Court. This was not a highly regarded position, but it helped Goya come to the attention of important artists.

Art boom

King Charles III was in power at this time and had ordered the building of a new Royal Palace, along with a number of churches and large mansions. This created a lot of work for artists who were commissioned to cover the buildings' walls with paintings and tapestries. Large woolen tapestries were especially popular as they helped keep out the cold and damp.

Tapestry production

As a tapestry designer, Goya would first sketch a design to be approved by the Court, and then paint it onto canvas, which was sent to tapestry weavers to copy. Goya's designs were often quite complicated. A work called *The Blind Guitarist* (below) was sent back by the weavers for him to redo, as it contained too many figures and different color tones for them to copy.

The Blind Guitarist, c.1778

Art

Look at the design and the tapestry of Blind Man's Buff. *What aspects of Goya's painting do you think have been lost in the final tapestry version?*

Blind Man's Buff painted design (left) and tapestry (right) c.1789

Spanish life

Royal officials decided the subjects of the tapestries. Traditionally these were images from myths or religious stories, but Goya started work at a time when scenes of present-day Spanish life were popular. These were generally light-hearted images showing both the wealthy and the poor at play. These subjects gave Goya an opportunity to develop his skill at capturing the interactions and behavior of people in groups. His tapestry design *The Parasol* (right) was created to decorate a royal dining room. It shows a wealthy young woman resting on the ground, with a small dog curled up in her lap. A possible male suitor stoops slightly behind, shading her from the sun by holding up a green parasol. However, the gaze of the woman suggests she is more interested in interacting with the viewer than she is the young man.

Gaining support

The German-born painter Anton Raphael Mengs (1728–1779) had been employed to oversee the decoration of the new Royal Palace and was impressed by Goya's tapestry designs. He encouraged Goya to apply for a position as a permanent painter in the Royal Court, and to become a member of the Royal Academy (see p.12–13).

The Parasol, c.1777

The Royal Academy

In 1776 and 1779, Goya applied for a job as Painter to the King. He was turned down both times, leaving him frustrated by his lack of progress. However, his luck changed in 1780 when he was elected as a member of the Royal Academy. This indicated that he was now seen as a serious and talented artist.

Gaining entrance

The Royal Academy was made up of Spain's top artists. They gave lectures and provided training and support to young artists. To gain membership Goya sent his painting of *Christ on the Cross* (below), which received a positive response from the Academy. The painting is traditional in its religious subject matter and shows the influence of Mengs and the Spanish painter Diego Velázquez (1599–1660).

Mengs

Mengs was one of the leading artists of a style known as Neoclassicism. This drew influences from Classical Greek and Roman sculpture, painting figures as if they were solid monuments. It was very different from the elaborate detail of Rococo art and is an approach that can be seen in both his and Goya's paintings of Christ on the cross. Goya's relationship with Mengs was important, not just for his influence in style, but also for gaining Goya access to the Royal Collection of paintings. Here, Goya was able to study masterpieces not available to the public.

Left: *Christ on the Cross*, 1780

Below: *Christ on the Cross*, Anton Raphael Mengs, 1769

Velázquez

Within the Royal Collection were many paintings by the artist Velázquez. He had been Spain's leading painter in the 17th century and was to be a huge influence on Goya. Velázquez sought to represent people as realistically and naturally as possible. Goya would go on to develop Velázquez's aims throughout his career. His *Christ on the Cross* (opposite, left) already showed Velázquez's influence – as well as copying the dark background from Velázquez's *Christ Crucified* (below), the expression and pose of Jesus is more tired and natural than heroic. Goya made a series of etchings (below, right) based on Velázquez's paintings from the Royal Collection, including Velázquez's *Portrait of Sebastian de Morra* (right). Morra was a dwarf and jester in the court of King Philip IV.

Portrait of Sebastian de Morra, Diego Velázquez, c.1645

Sebastian de Morra, c.1778.

Christ Crucified, Diego Velázquez, 1632

Self-portraits

Goya claimed that there were two artists that he considered his masters: Velázquez and the Dutch artist Rembrandt (1606–1669). Goya owned several etchings by Rembrandt. Like him, Goya was fascinated by contrasts of light and dark and wanted to capture expressions of character, often explored in his self-portraits.

Ageing in art

In their self-portraits, both artists often played around with ideas of what an artist should look like. Goya copied Rembrandt's images of the artist as a wild spirit (see portraits below), and both also painted themselves in different stages of old age and in ill health.

> "I see only forms that are lit up and forms that are not. There is only light and shadow." –Goya

Self-portrait, Rembrandt, c.1630

Light and mood

Goya was influenced by the way Rembrandt used contrasts of light and shadow in his artwork. Rembrandt often cast shadows across the face of his portraits to express the mood of the sitter. Goya uses extreme contrasts of shadows and light around his figures to create a more dramatic environment. In Goya's self-portrait *Self-portrait at the Easel* (opposite, top left) the artist stands alone in a half-silhouette against dazzling white light pouring through the window. This contrast places the artist as an observer in his own dark world, separate from the bright light and life outside.

Portraits of the artist

Goya's *Self-portrait at the Easel* bears similarities to Rembrandt's painting *The Artist in His Studio*, (opposite, top right) though he

Self-portrait, c.1798–1800

Self-portrait at the Easel, c.1790

The Artist in his Studio, Rembrandt, 1628

would not have seen Rembrandt's original. Both paintings present the artist as an heroic creator. In Rembrandt's painting the canvas and artist appear as opponents sizing each other up for battle. The artist is considering his work, stepping back at a distance that makes him appear much smaller than the canvas. Goya's painting conveys a similar message of battle, with the artist wearing a theatrical bullfighter's jacket.

Important people

Goya himself appears in his first important portrait commission, *Count Floridablanca* (right). In this painting, he is showing the Count his portrait, while the Count looks out toward a mirror to check its accuracy. This work was much admired and went on to earn Goya many more portrait commissions.

Count Floridablanca, 1783

Painter to the King

In 1786, Goya finally became Painter to the King, establishing himself in the Royal Court as an important artist. This status made him a fashionable painter and anyone who was anyone wanted to sit for a portrait by Goya, including the royal family, aristocracy and court officials.

Symbols

Goya's portraits often included symbols that gave clues to the status and life of the sitter. His painting of the Count of Altamira's son, Manuel (below), for example, features animals that represent the child's youth: the birds represent the child's innocence, while the wide-eyed cats suggest the evil lurking in the world.

Don Manuel Osorio de Zuñiga, c.1787

Character

Goya wanted to show his subjects realistically, as well as to capture their character. This often meant that the images were not very flattering. His paintings of King Charles III show him with a big nose and wrinkles around his eyes; however, he also looks kind and friendly.

Charles III in Hunting Costume, c.1786–88

Developing friendships and style

Many of Goya's patrons became his friends and are often painted in relaxed poses. One of his friends, the liberal minister and author Gaspar Melchor de Jovellanos, was painted in a thoughtful pose, without a wig (below). This was completed ten years after his portraits of Don Manuel and Charles III. It shows a development in Goya's style – his brushwork is looser, with no hard outlines around any of the objects.

Gaspar Melchor de Jovellanos, 1798

Alice Neel

Goya was a hero of the American painter Alice Neel (1900–1984). Neel specialized in painting portraits and, like Goya, tried to capture the character of her sitters. She noticed that Goya often explored variations of one color within his paintings, in particular silver and grey, something that she also explored in many of her paintings. This can be seen in Goya's portraits of Jovellanos and in Neel's portrait of the poet Frank O'Hara (below).

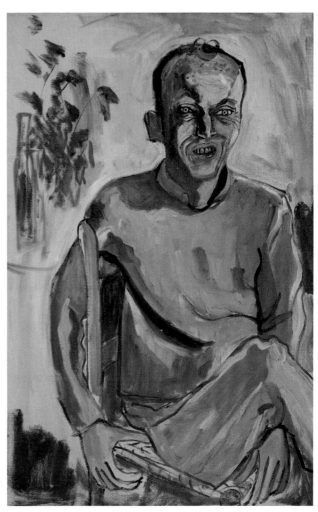

Frank O'Hara No. 2, Alice Neel, 1960

Art

The jumper and jacket in Goya's portrait of Jovellanos and Neel's portrait of Frank O'Hara each appear as one color, though they have been painted in a variety of different colors. What different colors can you spot?

17

Another world

In late 1792, while visiting a patron in Andalusia, Goya became very ill. For a while he was blind and unable to move. He was left deaf and only able to communicate by writing and using sign language. During his recovery, he created a series of dark paintings influenced by human suffering.

Cabinet paintings

It took Goya a year to recover from his illness, during which time he worked on a series of cabinet paintings. Cabinet paintings are small paintings, often of full-length figures, and were usually for display in study rooms. Goya's paintings had not been commissioned and were subjects of his own creation. They showed images of catastrophes and human desperation, perhaps reflecting his dark state of mind. The subjects included bullfights, people escaping a fire, a highway robbery, a shipwreck and an insane asylum. Many of these paintings came from his imagination, though he reported to have seen first-hand the violence and cruelty in *The Yard of a Mad House* (below, left).

Romanticism

Goya's dark images of disasters and suffering were unusual at this time but became more common in the early 19th century, in artwork produced by a movement known as Romanticism. Romantic artists rebelled against traditional subject matter, preferring to show ordinary people over aristocrats, and extreme emotions and violent acts of nature over a world of order and intellect.

The Yard of a Mad House, c.1793–4

The Shipwreck, c.1793–4

Théodore Géricault

A leading artist from the Romantic movement was the French painter Théodore Géricault (1791–1824). His painting *The Raft of the Medusa* (below) showed people struggling to survive following a disaster at sea. A similar theme appears in Goya's cabinet painting, *The Shipwreck* (opposite, right). However, Géricault's painting is based on a real shipwreck that occurred three years before his completed work. In an effort to get close to his subject he spent a long time making studies, building models, interviewing survivors as well as drawing drowned bodies. Like Goya, Géricault also visited insane asylums for subjects that appear in his later paintings.

The Raft of the Medusa, Théodore Géricault, 1818–19

Revolution

The events of the French Revolution (1789–1799) were taking place at the time of Goya's illness and also influenced many Romantic artists. This was a time of great political turmoil all over Europe, as people rebelled against set ideas of rules and representation. Goya was friends with many important liberal politicians in Spain and was sympathetic to political reforms that favored greater personal freedoms, rather than oppressive control under the state and Church. For Goya, liberty was a principle that should be applied to the arts as well as government. In 1792, in a speech at the Royal Academy, Goya declared that there were "no rules in painting," a shocking and bold statement that encouraged artists to move beyond the set ideas taught in art, promoting freedom of expression for all artists.

The Duchess and the *Maja*

Once Goya had recovered from his illness, he returned to painting portraits for the Royal Court. In private, he continued to produce artwork that expressed his dark imagination, as well as subjects that were not suitable for a public audience.

The Duchess of Alba

Goya became close to the Duchess of Alba, a famous figure in Madrid society. When her husband died in 1797, Goya went to stay with her. He made several sketches of her and painted a portrait (below) that led to rumours of them being lovers.

Dressed and undressed

Either during his stay with the duchess or shortly after, Goya began work on one of his most daring paintings, *La Maja Desnuda* ("the naked *maja*," *maja* being a fashionable young woman). It showed a woman lying naked on a sofa, staring invitingly toward the viewer. Some think that this may have been modelled on the duchess. Shortly after, he began work on *La Maja Vestida* ("the clothed *maja*"), which showed the same woman in the same pose, but this time fully clothed (opposite, top).

The *Maja Desnuda* painting was considered shocking for its overt nudity and was only the second such painting by a Spanish artist, after Velázquez's *Rokeby Venus* (1647–1651). Neither painting was shown publicly, and for a while both were kept in the private collection of the Spanish Prime Minister Godoy, one of Goya's patrons. Much later, in 1815, Goya was called before the Inquisition and questioned over who had commissioned them, but his explanation has never been brought to light.

Art

The Duchess of Alba wears two rings on her right hand; one has the name "Alba" inscribed on it, and the other the name "Goya." Her index finger points down to the ground where "Solo Goya" is written (meaning "only Goya"). Why do you think these details have been added?

The Duchess of Alba, 1797

La Maja Vestida, c.1800–1805

Madame X

The US painter and celebrated portraitist John Singer Sargent (1856–1925) was a fan of Goya, and both artists painted figures from wealthy society. Like Goya, Sargent also caused a scandal with a portrait of a woman. His painting *Madame X* (right) was thought to reveal too much flesh and Sargent had to repaint the shoulder straps of the dress so that it didn't appear as though the woman was undressing. Like the *La Maja Vestida*, it plays on the contrasts between white and black, here of the skin and dress, while Goya plays on the contrast of the white figure against the black background.

Madame X, John Singer Sargent, 1883–1884

Witches and demons

In 1798 Goya completed a series of six paintings showing scenes of witchcraft. Superstitious beliefs were common at this time, especially amongst the poor, where many believed in the existence of witches. These images also reflect the popularity of horror in the art and novels of northern Europe, with their influence creeping into Spain.

Horror

In countries such as England and Germany, audiences were keen to be scared by horror stories and paintings of supernatural beings. Many of these novels associated Catholicism with the terrors of ghosts and witches. Because of this, the Inquisition (see p.7) prevented such work becoming widely popular in Spain, although artists and their patrons would have been aware of their existence.

The Spell, 1797–1798

The Nightmare, Henry Fuseli, 1781

The Nightmare

A famous horror painting from around this period is *The Nightmare* (left), by Swiss painter Henry Fuseli (1741–1825). This shows a bad dream coming to life, a theme that haunts much of Goya's later work. It is very possible that Goya saw an engraving of this painting, as it was widely distributed throughout Europe.

Common beliefs

Witchcraft and superstition often appeared in Goya's private work. *The Spell* (opposite, top) shows a group of witches using a pin-prick doll and a spell book, summoning a spirit from above, as well as a witch reaching out for a victim to sacrifice. Goya was himself skeptical of witchcraft and superstition. He saw similarities between them and the power of the Inquisition – both inspired fear and involved rituals resulting in innocent deaths.

The Inquisition was known for holding witch trials where many innocent people were burned under the belief that they were witches. Goya addresses this in his painting *Witches' Flight* (right). Here, the witches appear as men, wearing hats that show they are to be burned alive by the Inquisition. However, the hats look like bishops' mitres, connecting the actions of the witches to the actions of the Church.

Witches' Flight, 1797–1798

Daring patrons

The Duke and Duchess of Osuna were two of Goya's most supportive patrons. They were fans of the fashion for horror, and bought Goya's paintings of witchcraft to hang in their private villa. They were part of a wealthy and powerful family and were able to protect favored artists from the Inquisition.

"I'm not afraid of witches, hobgoblins, apparitions, boastful giants [...] nor indeed any kind of beings except human beings..."
–Goya

23

Los Caprichos

Around the same time that Goya was producing his paintings of witchcraft, he was also creating a series of prints called *Los Caprichos*. They were published in 1799, but their subject matter led to them being withdrawn from sale.

Themes

In *Los Caprichos* Goya uses fantastical images to criticize the abuse of political and religious power in Spain, along with superstition. Themes include deception, transformation and being transported to another place. In *No. 39: And So Was His Grandfather* (below) a nobleman has been turned into an ass. He is looking at his family tree, which shows him as descended from a line of asses. *No. 61: They Have Flown* (below, right) shows a woman being carried off by three witch-like figures.

No. 39: And So Was His Grandfather, 1797–99

Technique

Within the series of 80 prints, Goya uses caricature, a technique that exaggerates certain features of a subject to make a point. He often makes his targets appear grotesque. The work shows off Goya's skill in etching and printmaking, particularly in his use of aquatint. This technique allowed him to block out areas in grey or black, creating a greater contrast between light and dark.

Recalled

Goya produced the prints himself and funded their production. However, within 15 days of their publication, he withdrew them from sale, fearful of a response from the Inquisition. A few copies had been bought and some made their way into France, which gained Goya greater fame abroad.

No. 61: They Have Flown, 1797–99

A monstrous nightmare

The most famous print from the series contains the phrase "The Sleep of Reason Produces Monsters" (right). It shows a man sleeping, while around him a nightmare of bat-like owls come to life to taunt him. Goya's message is that reason and intelligence must stay alert and awake in order to stand against the demons of stupidity and abuse of power.

No. 43: The Sleep of Reason Produces Monsters, 1797–1799

Art

How does Goya create a sense of nightmare in the The Sleep of Reason Produces Monsters, *while Redon's* A Psychedelic Dream *(below) has the sense of a dream?*

Odilon Redon

The French artist Odilon Redon (1840–1916) was greatly inspired by Goya and his flights of imagination. But while Goya's subjects were dark and nightmarish, Redon explored dreams as a means of an escape toward something more magical and beautiful. *The Sleep of Reason Produces Monsters* has become an iconic image of a nightmare come to life; Redon copied this composition in several paintings, but replaced the darkness with colorful dream-like images floating around the sleeper, as below.

The Sleep of Caliban, Odilon Redon, 1895–1900

The Family of Charles IV

One of the most important commissions for a Court Painter was to paint the royal family. When Charles IV and his wife María Luisa became king and queen of Spain in 1788, they were not well liked. Goya painted them and their family in 1800, creating a masterpiece that is seen as both grand and disrespectful.

Family fortunes

The royal family in France had just been removed from power and executed during the French Revolution, leaving monarchs all over Europe fearful of their futures. Goya was commissioned to paint the Spanish royal family as strong and united. He shows them in their finest clothes, decorated with jewels and medals (below). However, it is thought that by painting them in a realistic style, Goya chose not to flatter them, but to show their ugliness and vanity.

Las Meninas

Goya's portrait has clearly drawn on Velázquez's 1656 painting, *Las Meninas* (opposite, bottom), for inspiration. Velázquez's painting is of the family of King Philip IV, but it also features himself at work in the left of the image. Goya pays tribute to his hero by copying this feature, painting himself in the same position.

The Family of Charles IV, 1800

Playing with composition

By placing himself in the pose of Velázquez, Goya is inviting a direct comparison between the two paintings and their approach to royal portraiture. The title of Velázquez's painting translates as "The Maids of Honor," telling us that this is not meant as a royal family portrait, but a painting of the servants surrounding the young Princess Margaret Theresa. But this is above all a playful painting, and it features a royal portrait taking place within it – in the mirror on the background wall is the reflection of the king and queen, and it is them that Velázquez is looking out toward, painting them on his canvas.

A more formal portrait

The royal family is clearly present within Goya's painting, lined up stiffly in a row with the queen commanding the center of the group. But who is the Goya in the picture painting? If he is painting the royal family, then they must be standing in front of a large mirror, and he would be painting their reflection. Or perhaps he is painting the household staff that might be waiting in front of them, with the picture acting as an inverted version of Velázquez's painting. Or maybe he is staring out toward the audience who are looking at the painting, capturing their expressions as they gaze upon the royal family.

Las Meninas, Diego Velázquez, 1656

The Colossus

In 1808, French troops under the command of Emperor Napoleon Bonaparte marched across the French-Spanish border, attacking Spanish civilians and troops alike, and beginning what became known as the Peninsular War. During the following French occupation, Goya began work on one of his most famous paintings, *The Colossus*.

Giant battle

The Colossus (below), begun in 1808 and finished around 1812, shows a giant stomping through Spain with his fists raised. Beneath him a panicked crowd are fleeing in all directions. Many people interpret the figure of the colossus as representing the brutality of the French army, whereas some see him as a symbol of Spanish defiance in fighting back.

The Colossus, 1808–1812

Elegy to the Spanish Republic No. 131,
Robert Motherwell, 1974

Dark days

In *The Colossus*, dark colors that block out large parts of the canvas dominate the painting; flecks of white and a peach color have been applied on top with a palette knife. The overall effect is one of gloom and despair and may reflect Goya's attitude toward the war.

Goya's work?

Recently, some experts have called into question whether or not Goya painted *The Colossus* on his own or at all. At the bottom left are marks that resemble the letters "A J," the initials for his assistant at this time, Asensio Juliá. However, many other experts firmly believe that the painting is by Goya. It is quite different to his earlier work, but shows a crude style that he developed further in his *Black Paintings* (see p.38–39).

A poem for Spain

US artist Robert Motherwell (1915–1991) painted shapes that are not representative of real things, but present a mood or a sensation. In the 1960s he produced a series of large paintings called *Elegy to the Spanish Republic*, as a tribute to Spain and its troubled past. Motherwell had traveled across Spain as a young man and felt a strong connection to the country and to the work of Goya. He considered his use of black as connecting him to a tradition of painters, notably Goya, who used the color black freely. For Motherwell black is the color of funerals. In his paintings it dominates the canvas, as it does in Goya's *Colossus*.

Art *In* The Colossus, *people, horses and bulls are running away in all directions. Which symbolic creature is standing still and what do you think it might represent?*

The Disasters of War

Spanish liberals, including Goya, had at first welcomed the arrival of the French, hoping they would bring with them the reforming ideals of the Enlightenment. However, they were soon disillusioned as terrible violence spread across the country, with Spanish civilians fighting French soldiers. Goya was shocked by what he saw and expressed this in his art, producing a series of etchings that have had a huge impact on how artists show conflict in their work.

I Saw It, 1810–20

Disturbing truths

The Disasters of War is a series of 82 etchings that show gruesome images of people attacking each other, suffering and struggling to survive. Goya wanted to express as truthfully as possible the reality of war and so doesn't hide any details of violence, including acts of killing and the dead being carried away, as seen in *Cartloads to the Cemetery* (below). The series was not published until 1863, after Goya's death. It is possible that he kept them hidden for fear of trouble from both the French and Spanish authorities.

Cartloads to the Cemetery, 1810–20

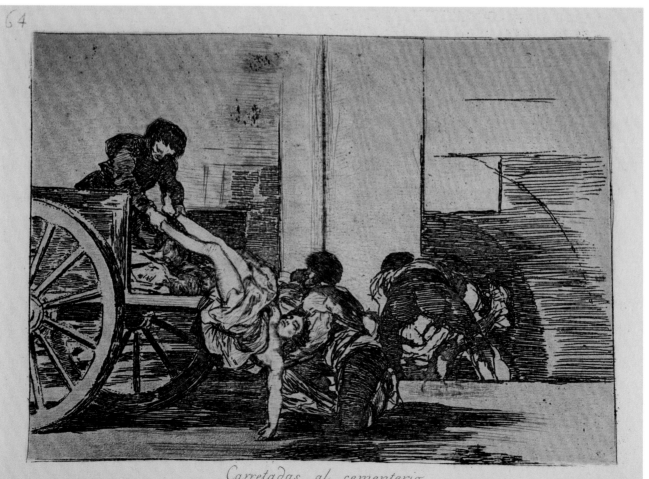

On no one's side

Up until this point, war art always showed one side as heroes defending their country. Goya instead showed both sides as equally brutal; he is not celebrating any country or army, but attacking man's inhumanity to man. Each print Goya produced is accompanied by a caption recording his experience. Under a scene of refugees fleeing from the French army (opposite, top) he wrote "I Saw It"; alongside a print of a dead man impaled on a tree with his arms cut off is the caption "This Is Worse."

Guernica

Spanish artist, Pablo Picasso (1881–1973), was given the nickname "*le petit Goya*" early in his career. Like Goya, Picasso shared an interest in Spanish culture and was moved to create work inspired by wars that took place in their home country.

Guernica, Pablo Picasso, 1937

In the 1930s Spain experienced a bloody civil war, where Nationalists loyal to the monarchy fought left-wing Republicans. During the conflict, a village called Guernica was bombed by German and Italian forces allied to the Nationalist cause. Over 1,600 civilians were killed. The Republicans commissioned Picasso to paint a work showing the atrocities of Guernica to show at the 1937 Paris World Fair and draw international attention to the Republican cause. The resulting work is considered one of the greatest paintings of the 20th century. It has become a powerful statement on the tragedy of war for the innocent and, like Goya's prints, it reflects the inhumanity of conflict.

> "The object of my work is to report the actuality of events."
> –Goya

Painting history

During the French occupation, Goya continued to work as court painter to the new French king, Joseph Bonaparte (brother to Napoleon). However, the French were soon defeated by a European alliance and the Spanish regained the throne. Goya's loyalty to Spain was called into question, and he sought to paint his way out of trouble.

The city of Madrid

Under French rule, Goya was selected to paint a portrait of the new king. He painted the *Allegory of the City of Madrid* (below), which originally featured the king's portrait in the medallion to the right. The painting is very different to his style at the time, recalling the Rococo influence from early in his career. Once Spanish rule was returned, the king's portrait was replaced by a portrait of King Ferdinand VII, and later by the date 2 May, a day when Spanish civilians rose up against French rule.

Loyalty

When the Spanish king Ferdinand VII returned to claim the throne, Goya was ordered to swear his love and allegiance to Spain or be considered a traitor to his country. To regain favor, he volunteered to produce history paintings to show Spanish victory against the French.

The 2nd of May, 1808

In 1814, Goya presented two paintings that commemorated the struggle of the Spanish civilians. They documented two important days; the first painting (opposite, top) shows the events of the 2nd of May, when the people of Madrid rose up against the French army. The chaos of the battle in this painting is thought to have been a big inspiration for the battle scenes painted by the French Romantic artist Eugène Delacroix (1798–1863).

Allegory of the City of Madrid, 1810

The 2nd of May 1808 in Madrid, 1814

Inside the action

Goya's painting has no single point of focus, with the battle spilling out over the edges of the painting. These were features picked up by Delacroix, in paintings such as *The Battle of Taillebourg* (right). This gives the impression that the images are not staged, but that the artists are recording it on the spot.

The Battle of Taillebourg, Eugène Delacroix, 1834–1835

The 3rd of May, 1808 in Madrid

The painting that accompanied *The 2nd of May 1808 in Madrid* showed a scene from the following day, when the French army had defeated the revolt, and rounded up Spanish citizens for execution. This was even more striking than its companion piece and has influenced many artists in representing scenes of war.

Art *Why do you think Goya chose to paint ordinary people involved in war?*

Power points

The power of this painting, *The 3rd of May, 1808 in Madrid*, comes from its contrasts in shapes and light and dark, as well as the expression of helplessness on the faces of the ordinary citizens being punished. Those facing the firing squad are lit up as if on a stage, surrounded by darkness. They are made up of rounded shapes that contrast with the strict row of soldiers and the hard lines of their rifles.

The Third of May, 1808 in Madrid, 1814

The Execution of Maximilian,
Edouard Manet, 1869

Legacy

The composition of *The Third of May in Madrid 1808* has been copied by many artists, using it to highlight the deaths of innocent citizens in conflicts all around the world. Artists inspired by this painting include George Bellows (1882–1925), Pablo Picasso, and most famously, the French artist Edouard Manet (1832–1883).

Further executions

In 1869, Manet painted *The Execution of Maximilian* (above), with a composition that pays direct reference to *The Third of May 1808 in Madrid*. Manet's painting shows the execution of the Austrian Archduke Ferdinand Maximilian by a firing squad. Maximilian was installed as the puppet ruler of a short-lived Mexican kingdom (1863–1867) by the French Emperor Napoleon III, who had invaded Mexico in 1861. He was captured by Mexican Nationalist forces and executed after the French armies withdrew in 1866. In Manet's painting the identity of the victims and executioners are the opposite to those featured in Goya's painting: here it is the Nationalists that are brutally executing representatives of the French invasion.

Follies

In 1815, Goya was called before the Inquisition to face questions over *La Maja Desnuda*. Little is known about the outcome of this trial, except he faced no harsh punishment. Around this time, Goya went into semi-retirement. He focused more on his increasingly mysterious and surreal private work.

The Burial of the Sardine

Goya's private paintings at this time showed a return to the subject of disturbing aspects of Spanish life, such as scenes from madhouses

The Burial of the Sardine, 1816

and violent religious celebrations. Among these works was *The Burial of the Sardine* (below, left), which showed a popular folk festival. Goya portrays it as a sinister event, showing excited figures with demonic forces hidden behind their carnival masks and costumes.

Further fantasy

Further scenes of a carnival nature appear in a series of prints Goya produced in between 1815–1823, known as *Los Disparates (The Follies)*. As well as depicting images from Spanish carnivals, they also play on proverbs and are filled with dark and dreamlike imagery. In *Disparate Volante (Flying Folly)* (below) a couple of lovers ride on a fantastic creature that is part-horse, part-bird. They're flying off into the dark unknown, but the creature's grotesque beaked head makes this seem like an image from a nightmare. Although it is unclear whether Goya had an overall meaning or purpose behind this series, some of the prints appear quite threatening and hint toward the political context of *Los Caprichos* (see p.24–25). *Bobalicón (Simpleton's Folly)* (opposite, top) has a priest placed alongside figures of fantasy –a giant grinning fool from a Spanish carnival

No. 5: Disparate Volante (Flying Folly), 1815–1823

No. 4: Bobalicón (Simpleton's Folly), 1815–1823

dances in front of him, with demons howling from out behind his back. It can be seen to show the Church retreating in fear from the jolly and sinister spirit of a peasant celebration. It may be that Goya felt these prints were too critical of Spanish society or too surreal for an audience, as the series was not printed until 1864, 36 years after his death.

Paula Rego

Paula Rego (1935–) is a Portuguese-born British artist who has been inspired by Goya's prints. This can be seen in her re-imaginings of traditional stories, sharing the same sense of the absurd in their depictions of reality. She also works in print, and has etched series on nursery rhymes, famous stories and even Disney films. She recasts them into adult worlds where they appear surreal and sinister, similar to Goya's *Los Disparates* prints.

There Was a Man of Double Deed (Nursery Rhyme series), Paula Rego, 1989

The *Black Paintings*

In 1819, Goya bought a house on the outskirts of Madrid known as "The House of the Deaf Man." At around the same time he fell seriously ill. On his recovery, Goya began decorating his new home with his most bleak and famous series of works, known as the *Black Paintings*.

Death's door

We don't know what illness had affected Goya, but it appeared to be life-threatening. He produced a painting called *Self-portrait with Dr. Arrieta* (below) which recorded his recovery. He gave the painting to his doctor as a thank-you gift.

Self-portrait with Dr. Arrieta, 1820

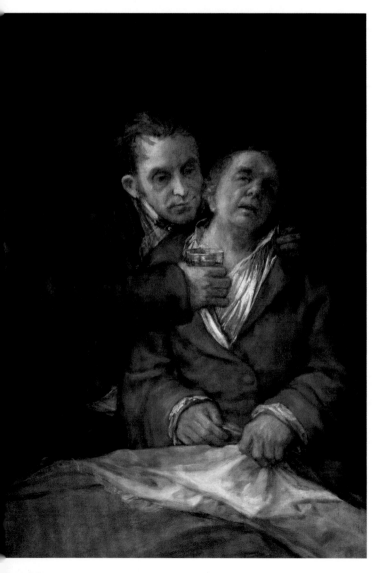

Old man, new tricks

Following his illness, Goya shut himself away from the world and began painting directly onto the walls of his new house. Known as the *Black Paintings* because of their heavy use of dark tones, these works have been interpreted as reflections on the cruelty of illness, old age and the political chaos in Spain. They express a gloomy state of mind and yet also show a renewed burst of inspiration and vitality, with Goya exploring an expressive style of painting.

The Dog, c.1820

A Pilgrimage to St. Isidore, 1820–1823

Subject

The series was named after Goya's death, when they were transferred onto canvas. There are 14 paintings in total, of subjects including witchcraft, old age and a dog sinking into quicksand (opposite, bottom). The sense of gloom and despair can be found in *A Pilgrimage to St. Isidore* (above). It shows a snake-like procession of groaning figures. As with the rest of the *Black Paintings*, they are figures trapped in torment, with little sign of rescue.

Technique

The paintings were created with heavy, thick dabs of paint using brushes or a palette knife. Some experts even think he threw paint violently against the wall.

Expressionism

The *Black Paintings* are often considered as a forerunner to a 20th century art movement known as Expressionism. This movement looked to present emotional experiences through a distorted physical reality. The Expressionists used heavy brushstrokes to show feelings of anger and sorrow. A famous early Expressionist painting is *The Scream*, by Edvard Munch (1832–1944). Here, the artist's expression of despair is

The Scream, Edvard Munch, 1893

screaming out through the figure's pose, the surrounding swirling brushstrokes and the burning orange sky.

Final flourishes

In 1823 Ferdinand VII was restored to the Spanish throne. He immediately set about taking bloody revenge on those who had opposed him, including liberals. Goya was horrified by the new violence, and moved to France to live out his last years.

Positive productivity

The artworks Goya produced in France show less of the gloom of his *Black Paintings*. Although he filled sketchbooks with images of haggard old women, prisoners and beggars, he also produced paintings that recalled some of the light and color of his earlier work. Even though he was an old man of 78, had suffered terrible illnesses and had failing eyesight, Goya was still exploring new ways of making art. His creative energy is summed up in his drawing of an old man supporting himself with two walking sticks moving forward (right). It is called *Aun Aprendo*, meaning "I'm still learning." Though not a self-portrait, it shows Goya's refusal to let old age put a stop to his work.

Lithography

Around this time, Goya became the first major European artist to experiment with the technique of lithograph printing. More like drawing than engraving, it involves preparing a smooth surface, such as a stone, onto which the ink is applied. The final image appears when paper is pressed up against

Aun Aprendo, (I'm Still Learning), 1824–1828

the surface. Goya made a series of lithograph prints on the subject of one of his favorite pastimes – bullfighting. This series, created in 1825 and known as the *Bulls of Bordeaux*, show the bullfight from a distance, placing the viewer as a spectator, away from the dangerous act of bullfighting (below).

Bullfight in a Divided Ring, 1825

Art *Compare* Bullfight in a Divided Ring *to the etched prints on p.30–31. What differences do you notice in the quality of line?*

The Milkmaid of Bordeaux

Goya continued to paint portraits, but not of wealthy aristocrats. He was more interested in recording the lives of ordinary people. His most famous painting from this period is *The Milkmaid of Bordeaux* (right). The paint was applied with a combination of brush, palette knife and rag, with the shape of the milkmaid formed by painted flecks marking out areas of light. Many experts have called this the first painting of Impressionism.

The Milkmaid of Bordeaux, 1825–1827 (and detail, left)

The outline of the milkmaid's shawl is created by intermittent marks of paint that look like dappled light.

Impressionism

Impressionism is an art movement that appeared around 50 years after Goya's death. The Impressionists were a group of mainly Paris-based artists who painted scenes of ordinary life. They were named by an art critic after a painting by Claude Monet (1840-1926) entitled *Impression, Sunrise* (1872). The Impressionists painted quickly, in the hope of capturing the image in front of them before it disappeared. Impressionist painters, such as Camille Pissarro (1830–1903), applied rapid brushstrokes to highlight the fleeting appearance of light and movement. The effect was to leave visible brush marks, much like those seen in Goya's *The Milkmaid of Bordeaux*.

The Shepherdess, Camille Pissarro, 1881

A modern visionary

Goya died on April 16, 1828 and was buried in a church in Bordeaux. It took several years before his work was widely seen and its brilliance recognized. Sixty years after his death, Goya's remains were reburied in Madrid. The country he had loved and criticized wanted him back, and now celebrates him as a national treasure.

Discovery

After Goya's death the work that he had produced in private gradually began to be seen all over the world. This work sheds a light on life in Spain during a period of political turmoil, with images that ask us to question what we see. His tapestry design *Little Giants* (below) has a bright and playful subject matter, but also fascinates us with the possibility of something

more sinister – up close the main child has shark-like teeth, and his legs are gripped tightly around the other boy's neck. *Two Old Men* (below) shows a grotesque clergyman shouting into an old man's ear – perhaps hinting at Goya's own deafness and the presence of the Inquisition in Spain.

Modern influence

Goya's vast range of subjects and styles can be traced in many modern art movements. These include the drama and darkness of Romantic artists, the fantastical worlds of Surrealism, the representations of feelings explored by Expressionism, and the forms of light captured by the Impressionists. Throughout his career Goya sought to express reality, particularly in showing people and their behavior. His search for new ways of expression has made him a hero to many important modern artists, such as

Little Giants, 1791

Two Old Men, 1819–1823

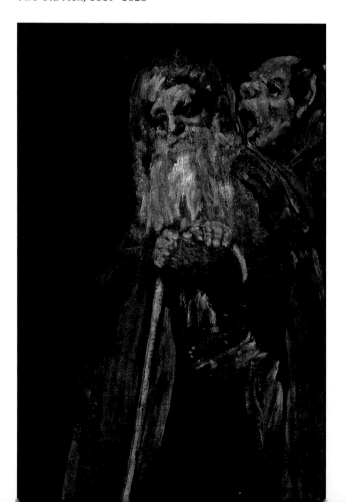

Untitled, Ahmed Alsoudani, 2008

Edouard Manet, Salvador Dalí and Pablo Picasso. These artists in turn have developed Goya's visions and changed the way we see art, and the world around us.

A continuing legacy

Goya's influence can be seen in the work of Iraqi-born painter Ahmed Alsoudani (1975–), where the presence of war is formed through mashed-up fragments of information and personal experience. His images recall the violence and mutilations of *The Disasters of War* (see p.30–31), with forms twisting around like Goya's grotesque witches and demons. Like Goya, Alsoudani is seeking to express his own feelings of horror through a new visual language. It is this use of art to express the unspeakable that makes Goya an artist ahead of his time and a continuing inspiration.

Timeline

1746 March 30, Goya is born in Fuendetodos, Spain

1749 Goya and family move to nearby city, Saragossa

1759 Charles III becomes King of Spain

1760 works as apprentice to José Luzán

1764 moves to Madrid and studies under Francisco Bayeu

c.1769–71 studies in Italy

1771 enters painting *The Victorious Hannibal* into completion in Italy

returns to Saragossa

c. 1772 completes *The Adoration of the Name of God*

1773 marries Josefa Bayeu

1775 begins work as tapestry designer

birth of his second child

1778 completes tapestry design *The Blind Guitarist*

works on series of etchings of Velázquez paintings

1780 becomes a member of the Royal Academy of San Fernando, entering his painting *Christ on the Cross* to gain membership

1783 paints *Count Floridablanca*, his first important commission

1784 birth of his seventh child, Javier, only one of his children to reach adulthood

1785 appointed Assistant Director of Painting at the Royal Academy

1786 becomes Painter to the King

c.1786–88 paints *Charles III in Hunting Costume*

c. 1787 paints *Don Manuel Osorio de Zuñiga*

1788 Charles III dies; Charles IV becomes King of Spain

1789 beginning of the French Revolution

c.1790 paints *Self-portrait with Easel*

1792 becomes seriously ill

1793–94 works on series of cabinet paintings

1795 becomes director of the Royal Academy

1797 paints *The Duchess of Alba*

c.1798–1800 paints *La Maja Desnuda*

c.1798–1805 paints *La Maja Vestida*

1798 six witchcraft paintings sold to the Duke and Duchess of Osuna

paints *Gaspar Melchor de Jovellanos*

1799 becomes the First Court Painter

publishes *Los Caprichos* but withdraws them from sale 15 days later

1800 paints *The Family of Charles IV*

1808 Spanish royal family abandon throne

French army invade Spain

Joseph Bonaparte becomes French King of Spain

1808–12 paints *The Colossus*

1810 Inquisition is suppressed

begins work on *The Disasters of War*

paints *Allegory of the City of Madrid*

1812 French are defeated by an alliance of European forces led by Britain's General Wellington

death of Goya's wife, Josefa

1814 Ferdinand VII restored as king of Spain

paints *The Second of May 1808 in Madrid* and *The Third of May 1808 in Madrid*

1815 Inquisition reinstated

Goya is brought before the Inquisition

c.1816 paints *The Burial of the Sardine*

1817 begins work on *Los Disparates*

1819 moves into "The House of the Deaf Man"

becomes seriously ill

1820 paints *Self-portrait with Dr. Arrieta*

begins work on the *Black Paintings*

1823 Goya leaves Spain for France, visits Paris, but settles in Bordeaux

1825 begins working in lithography and produces the series *The Bulls of Bordeaux*

c.1825–27 paints *The Milkmaid of Bordeaux*

1826 returns to Madrid to request a full pension and pose for official portrait for the Royal Academy

1828 April 16, Goya dies and is buried in cemetery in Bordeaux, France

1901 at the request of the Spanish government, Goya's remains are dug up and reburied in the church of San Antonio de la Florida in Madrid, Spain

Selected works

Background information on some
of Goya's works:

The Victorious Hannibal Seeing Italy from the Alps for the First Time, 1771 (p.8)

Hannibal was a military leader from ancient history who, with his army from Carthage (modern-day Tunisia in North Africa), crossed the Alps into Italy to fight the Romans. In Goya's painting, Hannibal is seen lifting his helmet, glimpsing Italy for the first time. The figure with the bull's head in the bottom left of the painting represents the River Po, a famous river that he crossed as a point of no return in going forward into battle. A winged spirit accompanies Hannibal and there is a flying chariot in the background, placing the event into a mythological world, as well as one from history.

Self-portrait with Easel, c.1790 (p.15)

This portrait shows Goya's use of contrasts both with light and dark, and in his application of brushstrokes. The dark background and reddish-brown coat contrast with his white shirt and pale face. The dark blocks of color have been painted energetically with loose brushwork, while the face appears more sensitively captured with finer brushstrokes. These contrasts highlight the vulnerability of Goya at this stage in his life. The face of the artist glows out of the surrounding darkness with the soft and sagging skin of old age. The painting shows Goya with candle-holders around the rim of his hat. These held candles that he would have lit when he was working late at night. He preferred to work at night with his canvases illuminated by artificial light. His son later noted that:

"He painted only in one session, sometimes of ten hours, but never in the late afternoon. The last touches for the better effect of a picture he gave at night, by artificial light."

Count Floridablanca, 1783 (p.15)

Count Floridablanca was the chief minister of King Charles III. Both the count and Goya liked to work late into the night, as seen by the time on the clock (10.30 pm). The painting is filled with symbols to show both figures as important talents. Plans for a canal are leaning against the table and the floor is a book on the techniques of painting. These items show the count as skilled and knowledgeable in engineering and the arts. Goya is keen to make his presence felt in Court portraiture. As well as placing himself in the painting, by his feet is a notebook with his name written in it. Above both the count and Goya is a portrait of King Charles III, looking down on them with a look of approval at their work.

Allegory of the City of Madrid, 1810 (p.32)

The figure pointing to the medallion represents the city of Madrid; she is introducing the new king to his citizens, the audience who would have seen the painting in the town hall where it was displayed. The introduction is accompanied by music being played by the surrounding angels. Over the years the space within the medallion, where Joseph's portrait was originally placed, has been painted over several times, featuring different portraits and messages left by different artists.

Self-portrait with Dr. Arrieta, 1820 (p.38)

Upon his recovery from his illness, Goya painted this portrait of himself being nursed back to health by his doctor. We do not know what the illness was, but it was clearly serious; the painting contains Goya's inscription at the bottom, dedicated to the doctor:

"in gratitude for his success and great care he has taken saving my life during the violent and dangerous illness I suffered in late 1819, at the age of seventy-three."

The painting shows Goya weak and in pain, supported by the doctor, but surrounded by mysterious figures in the darkness behind them. These ghostly specters appear almost like a sign of the grotesque figures that were soon to overtake his imagination and cover the walls of Goya's house in his *Black Paintings*.

Glossary

Age of Enlightenment a period in European history, from around 1650–1780, when many scientists, writers and thinkers began to place reason above tradition and question established beliefs, such as the authority of the Church and the monarchy

allegory a picture or story that contains a hidden meaning which is often political

apprentice a person who is learning a new skill or job by working for an expert in that profession

aquatint a print that resembles the washes achieved with watercolors by a process that allows for several tones to be produced, using a copper plate etched with nitric acid

aristocracy the highest class of people in society, usually people born into wealth and who have titles such as Duke and Duchess

caricature representation of a person for comic effect, by exaggerating parts of their body, behavior or facial features

catastrophe an event or disaster that causes great damage and suffering

civilian A person who is not in the army

colossus a thing or person of enormous size

commission where a person or an organization asks an artist to produce work in return for paying a fee

composition how all the elements of an image, such as a painting, fit together

conflict a disagreement that has led to a violent struggle or even full-scale war

contrast a striking difference between two things, such as between darkness and light

deception the action of tricking someone and not telling them the truth

depiction a representation of something made in a drawing or painting

despair the loss or complete absence of hope

elegy a poem or song that offers reflection on the dead

engraving a print made from an inked block that has had a design etched or painted onto it

etching a print made from a block or plate that has had a design etched onto it

Expressionism a style of art that seeks to express the world of emotions rather than the physical world

flattering to praise someone, sometimes to make them appear more attractive than they really are

formal in accordance with rules or ceremony

French Revolution an uprising in France against the ruling monarchy, from 1789–1799, that resulted in the establishment of France as a republic

frescos paintings completed on wet plaster directly onto a wall or ceiling

gilder a person who adds gold decoration to frames and church altarpieces

glaze a thin covering with a smooth and shiny surface

grotesque something that looks very ugly, almost unnatural and sometimes comical

Impressionism an art movement, formed in France in the mid-19th century, that was interested in capturing the impression of movement and its shifting effects of light and color

informal relaxed and friendly, the opposite of formal

inhumanity extremely cruel and brutal behavior

Inquisition a special court that was set up to protect the interests of Catholicism in Spain

inverted arranged in the opposite position; turned upside down

legacy a gift or accomplishment that has been left behind by someone who has died

liberal someone who is open to new ideas, who favors political and social reform and greater freedom for individuals, as opposed to control by the government or monarchy

liberty freedom

lithography a process of printing from a smooth stone or plate that has a design drawn onto its inked surface

loyalty being faithful to family, friends or country

monarchy kings and queens that are the head of a country

naturalism a representation of the natural appearance of someone or something, presenting them as they appear realistically and not as how they may wish to be seen

Neoclassicism a style of art that developed in the mid-18th century that looked to the shapes and forms of Greek and Roman statues for influence in the representation of objects as solid and monumental

Old Masters great artists from the 16th–18th centuries

oppressive cruel and unjust

patron a person who buys works of art or supports an artist or a cause

Peninsular War a war from 1808–1814, fought in the Iberian Peninsula (Portugal and Spain) by British, Portuguese and Spanish forces against the French

pose the deliberate positioning of the person's body for a painting or drawing

prestigious a position of high status and respect

proverb a saying that contains a commonly believed truth or piece of advice

publication to make a printed work available

realism an attempt in art or literature to be true to life as we know it, not as we might wish or imagine it to be

reign period of rule of a king or queen

Rococo a highly decorative style of art and design that was popular in Europe in the 18th century

Romanticism a movements in the arts from the late 18th and early 19th centuries that sought to rebel against traditional expectations of art, showing an interest in dramatic expressions of emotion and imagination

scholarship money given to support a student's education

sinister to give the impression of something evil or criminal

surreal showing something dreamlike and unfamiliar; having come from the unconscious mind or from a dream

Surrealism an artistic movement from the 20th century that looked to express the creativity of the unconscious mind

symbol an object used to represent something which cannot be seen, such as an idea or feeling

tapestry a piece of fabric with pictures woven or embroidered on top, often used for hanging on walls

tones the shades of color within a picture

traditional a way of doing something, behaving and thinking that has been in use for a long period of time

traitor a person who shows disloyalty toward a person or a country, such as by helping or supporting an enemy

translucent a surface that is clear enough to allow light to pass through

tribute an act or a gift that is meant to show appreciation and admiration for someone or something

vanity excessive pride in oneself

For More Information

Books:

Artists Through the Ages: Francisco Goya by Alix Wood (Windmill Books, 2013)

Goya by Enriqueta Harris (Phaidon Press, 1998)

Goya: His Life and Works in 500 Images by Susie Hodge (Lorenz Books, 2015)

Websites

Because of the changing nature of Internet links, Rosen Publishing has developed an online list of websites related to the subject of this book. This site is updated regularly. Please use this link to access this list:

http://www.rosenlinks.com/ART/Goya

Index